The Big City and How It Grew

THE BIG CITY SERIES

CATHERINE URELL, PH.D.
Bureau of Educational Research
Board of Education, City of New York

ANNE JENNINGS
Reading Consultant
Board of Education, City of New York

FLORENCE R. WEINBERG
Classroom Teacher
Board of Education, City of New York

FOLLETT PUBLISHING COMPANY

New York   CHICAGO   *Los Angeles*

A note to the teacher appears on pages 123-27.

Everything we see in our big city has its history — churches, schools, bridges, city departments. Changes occur every day in New York, but the past is still very much with us. In this book Mr. Park's class learns about **the big city and how it grew.**

After seeing a picture of old Erasmus Hall, Kay asks, "How did New York grow so big?" Turn to page 6 to find out **how the unit started.**

The children discuss how the Dutch built and ruled the city. Start **then the white man came** on page 11.

What happened after the Dutch ruled our city? The children take up **New York as an English colony.** Begin on page 23.

Ann's committee made a report on trouble between the colonies and England. Begin **the Revolutionary War in New York** on page 33.

The Revolutionary War is over! But new problems have to be met. See page 39 for the story of New York after the Revolution.

What was New York like **a hundred years ago?** Manhattan and Brooklyn still had many countrylike things. See page 61.

People in **New York after the Civil War** saw many changes. Transportation, communication, education were changing fast, as were other things. Turn to page 71.

Mike's grandfather tells about an exciting time — **the turn of the century.** He also tells them how Greater New York began. See page 81.

In **the meaning of history** the children learn how many different peoples have their part in our city's history. Start on page 95.

Mr. Park tells the class some things that happened when he was growing up. Begin his story of **what happened day before yesterday** on page 107.

The children tell how **today came from yesterday.** They discuss the boroughs of New York and what they like about each, starting on page 109.

The children make a display of the old and the new in their city. They agree that **New York tomorrow** will be a wonderful place to live in. See page 119.

How the Unit Started

Mr. Park's children were walking along the street,
just looking at the buildings. They looked up
at a big high school called Erasmus Hall. Flo, Kay,
and Tim suddenly stopped at the entrance.

What did they see through
the arch? "Look!" Flo cried.
"There's a smaller building
in the courtyard."

"That's old Erasmus Hall,"
said Harry. "It was built
long ago, even before
Washington was president.
My dad told me about it.
He says everybody
in the school loves
the old building."

"I have a picture of the building in its early days," said Mr. Park. "I'll show it to you when we get back to school.

"That old church across the street is almost as old as the school. It stands where the first church on Long Island stood."

The children looked at the church and school. Then they looked at the other modern buildings.

Back at school, Mr. Park showed the children his picture of old Erasmus Hall. Then Kay asked, "How did New York City grow so big?"

"We studied about that last year," said Tim. "First the Indians lived here. Then the Dutch came. They built the city."

"Didn't anything happen after the Dutch built their city?" asked Mr. Park.

Tim looked surprised. Then he laughed. "I guess a lot happened between then and now," he said. "Could we find out about it all?"

"If you would like to," said Mr. Park. "We could take some trips. We could collect some pictures of old New York."

"Let's start with Erasmus Hall," Harry said. "We learned all about the Indians and the Dutch last year."

"Well, first let's see how well you remember what you learned about the Indians," said Mr. Park. These are the things the children remembered:

Indian Days

The Indians of this region lived in dome-shaped huts, called wigwams. Each wigwam was covered with bark. Inside, in the middle, a fire was built. The smoke went out through a hole in the top of the wigwam.

The Indians had to work hard to be sure of food all the year round. They had no stores to buy from if their food ran out. The women planted corn, beans, squash, and pumpkins. They had to watch out for crows and other birds that wanted to pick the seeds out of the ground. The children often had the job of driving the birds away. The women dried the beans and corn to eat in the winter. They pounded the corn to make cornmeal.

It was the men's job
to hunt and fish. The women
cut up the meat and cooked it.
They tanned the deerhide
and softened it up so that
it would make warm clothing.
They sewed the clothing
with fishbone needles.
They trimmed the best clothes
with porcupine quills dyed
with pretty colors.

Every spring, then as now, great numbers of shad
swam up the Hudson. The men strung nets across
the river to catch these delicious fish. It was
their job to mend the nets every spring. They had
to make boats used for shad fishing and for travel
and trading. The women had to smoke all the shad
that wasn't eaten at once. The smoked shad was
put away to eat in winter when other foods were hard
to get. Why were the shad good to eat all winter?

Then the White Man Came

"You remembered a good deal about the Indians," said Mr. Park. "Do you know what white man first brought a ship into New York harbor?"

"I know!" cried Maria. "It was Verrazano, and he was Italian, like me. Papa took me to visit his statue in Battery Park. It's too bad Verrazano didn't bring settlers."

"Families didn't come here to live until a hundred years after Verrazano's voyage," said Mr. Park.

"The next visitor didn't bring settlers either. He was Henry Hudson, an Englishman who was captain of a Dutch ship, the *Half Moon*. Near Coney Island, he sent some men ashore to get fresh drinking water. The Indians living there were scared. One of them shot an arrow and killed a sailor named Coleman. Some people think that Coney Island was once called Coleman Island, because of this sailor who was buried there. Others think it was named for the rabbits that people hunted there, since coney is another name for rabbit."

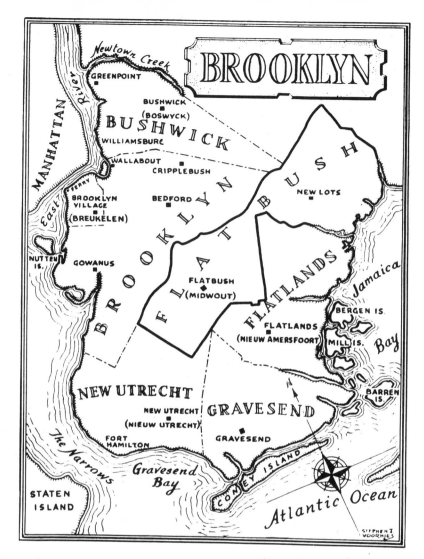

"I'm going to keep this map on our bulletin board
for a while. It shows the entrance to New York harbor
and it shows Brooklyn. Can you find Coney Island?

"Because of Hudson's voyage, the Dutch claimed
the land around New York Bay and along the Hudson River.
Dutch fur traders began coming here soon, to trap
fur-bearing animals in winter.

"Before long, a group of businessmen called
the Dutch West India Company decided to send families
here to live. The company was in charge of the colony
and was to send governors for it.

"Most of the first settlers went up the Hudson to live at Fort Orange. This fort was near the place where the Mohawk River flows into the Hudson. It was a good place for trading with the Indians, who followed trails along the Mohawk Valley when they brought furs to sell.

"The Mohawk Valley has always been important to the people of New York. Today, a canal, a railroad, and a highway follow this valley. Why are valleys good for transportation lines?

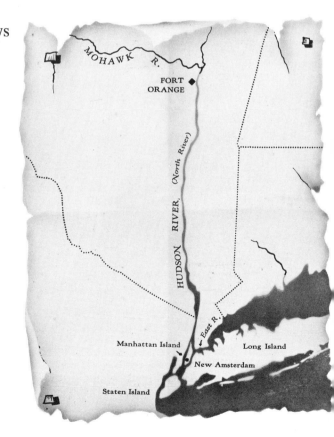

"The families at Fort Orange stayed there a little more than two years. They left because of Indian troubles. Their captain had taken sides in an Indian war, so the settlement became a dangerous place to live in.

"The settlers went back down the Hudson to Manhattan, where there was a newer, but larger, Dutch settlement. It was called New Amsterdam."

Mr. Park's class told these stories of the Dutch:

What About Indian Troubles?

The Indians were helpful to the fur traders. They were friendly people, and they liked the goods the white men traded for their furs. They taught the Dutch traders how to hunt or trap the animals they needed for fur. They taught the settlers how to grow corn and beans together and how to make the soil rich by planting fish along with the seeds.

Indian children taught Dutch boys and girls their games and showed them the secrets of the forest. Probably the Dutch children taught their Indian friends how to skate on ice.

Dutch preachers tried to teach their religion to the Indians, but the Indians were not interested. However, they were interested in the white men's tools. Steel knives and axes would make life in the woods much easier. Sharp steel needles and iron kettles would help Indian women with their work. Summer clothes of cloth were cooler than deerskin ones. Perhaps the Indians learned to like foods from the Dutch gardens — beets, spinach, parsley, and watermelons.

Some of the white men were fair to the Indians, but others were not. Fur traders found that they could get fine furs cheaper by paying for them with rum, guns, or gunpowder. The Indians liked the weapons of the white man and also enjoyed the white man's drink.

As time went on, there were quarrels between the Dutch and the Indians. The two groups were different in their customs and in their knowledge. They did not understand what trouble they were making for each other. For instance, the white farmers did not fence in their cows, and the cows strayed into the Indians' cornfields. The white men cut down trees to clear land for planting or to get wood to use in building.

The Indians got angry about their cornfields and their hunting grounds. Most of them quietly moved away. That did no good. The white man kept moving farther and farther into Indian lands. He usually paid for his land, but the Indians did not know what it meant to sell their land.

The worst quarrels happened because the Indians and the Dutch had different ideas about punishment. The Dutch thought that a person guilty of a crime should be punished. But the Indians thought that if a person did something wrong, all his people were guilty. His tribe should have brought him up to do right. When a white man killed an Indian, it was right for an Indian to kill a white man. Any white man would do, because the whole Dutch "tribe" was to blame.

Who Were the Dutch Governors?

New Amsterdam was the capital and the largest town
in the Dutch colony. It had thirty-one houses
when the Dutch from Fort Orange came there to live.

Peter Minuit, the governor of the colony, lived there.
He had bought Manhattan Island from the Indians. He had
paid for it with white men's goods the Indians wanted.

But New Amsterdam was only a settlement
at the lower end of Manhattan. It was not the entire
Dutch colony. In all the country round about,
Dutch people lived on farms far from one another,
but all the same they were part of the colony. The colony
was called New Netherland, because the home country
of the Dutch was called the Netherlands.

The Youngest Governor

Wouter van Twiller came after Minuit as governor
of New Netherland. He was young for a governor,
not yet thirty years old. He ordered some important
new buildings for New Amsterdam — a bakery, a church,
and a government house. He bought Governor's Island,
which was named for him. Before, it had been called
Nut Island.

In 1638 he had a little farmhouse
built for him in Flatlands, now part
of Brooklyn. It is still standing
today, probably the oldest house
in New York City. The smaller part
at the far end is the old part.
The slope of the roof was like that
of most Dutch farmhouses.

Some people in the colony though Van Twiller
was too lazy to be a good governor. They wanted him
to be sent back to the Netherlands, and so he was.
He never returned to enjoy his little house, but he
was not forgotten. The Indians remembered him, for he had
been their friend and had tried to understand them.

The Governor Who Hated Indians

It was bad luck for everybody that an old trouble
started up again soon after Willem Kieft became governor.
An Indian killed a white man to get even for a murder
committed long ago. The Indians were asked to give up
the guilty man. They would not, because they felt
he had done right.

Then Kieft did a dreadful thing. He ordered
his soldiers to attack an Indian village while
the Indians were sleeping. Men, women, and children
were murdered. Those who escaped cried out
for Van Twiller, "Wouter! Wouter!"

A serious war followed. Some of Kieft's advisers
were wiser than he. They trusted the Indians,
and the Indians trusted them. Two of them visited
the enemy, stayed overnight, and brought back
some Indian chiefs with them to talk about peace.
After many delays, caused by Kieft, peace was made.

Meanwhile, the Indians had killed or kidnapped
farmers and burned farm buildings. They did not
attack New Amsterdam, because of its fort.
But everywhere else they used the guns and gunpowder
so foolishly traded to them. The rum made them
even more savage than they usually were in war.

There were fewer people in the colony when the war ended than when Kieft first came. The land north of Manhattan had suffered badly. In this picture we see Jonas Bronck making a peace treaty with the Indians. What borough was named for him?

Kieft was ordered back to the Netherlands. But he never got there, because his ship was wrecked.

We must not think of Kieft as all bad. He tried to improve New Amsterdam. For one thing, he had a big inn built. Not only visitors stayed there, but also settlers waiting for their homes to be built.

Kieft bought the land that is now Queens.

The finest thing about Kieft is that he let people worship God as they thought was right.

"Old Silvernails"

The last and greatest governor of New Amsterdam was Peter Stuyvesant. He had many nicknames, which all had to do with his wooden leg. It was bound together with silver bands, fastened with silver nails. He had lost his leg as a fighter for his country, and a fighter he always was.

For the most part, Stuyvesant kept peace with the Indians. It was harder to keep peace with the Dutch. You see, Stuyvesant was a born boss. Many of his ideas were good, but the people wanted to think things out for themselves.

So the people in New Amsterdam and the towns on Long Island demanded more chance to govern themselves. In 1653, more than 300 years ago, New Amsterdam got a charter that gave it city government. Kieft's inn became the city hall. Before long, eleven villages on Long Island, five Dutch and six English, had their own governments. Of course, Stuyvesant was still the most powerful person in New Netherland.

Stuyvesant made rules to protect the towns from fires. Wooden chimneys caused many fires, especially when they were not kept clean. Stuyvesant supplied rattles for the night watchmen, so that people might be warned of fires or robbers. His watchmen were called the Rattle Watch.

He ordered people to fence
in their pigs and cows
and to repair their buildings.
He ordered pavements
for some streets. The first
street that was paved
was called Stone Street,
and is so called to this day.
Here we see men working
on the paving job.

Stuyvesant had a wall built north of New Amsterdam.
Today's Wall Street was first a path along this wall.
The wall was built to protect the town from warlike
Indians and from the English. You see, settlers
from near-by English colonies were moving into
New Netherland. They liked the Dutch way of not meddling
with people's ways of living and believing. But they
also liked the Dutch lands, and Stuyvesant was afraid
they might try to take over New Netherland.

These two pictures show you Manhattan then and now.

Freedom of Religion

The Dutch West India Company expected the colony to have freedom of religion. But Stuyvesant wanted the Dutch Church and no others. He hated the Quaker religion, especially. Quakers were as sure that they were right as *he* was sure that they were wrong.

Long Island had many settlements of English people from near-by colonies or from the old country. One of these settlements, Flushing, had people who gave Stuyvesant a good deal of trouble. They were kind and gentle toward believers in any religion.

The man who troubled Stuyvesant most was John Bowne. Bowne was a Quaker, and he had built a house in Flushing that was a fine place for meetings. So he invited Quakers to meet there.

For this, Stuyvesant threw him into jail. Bowne would not give in. Stuyvesant let him go home for a visit, hoping he would run away. But Bowne came back to jail. Then Stuyvesant banished him from the colony. What did Bowne do? He went to the Netherlands, told his story, and won the right of freedom of religion for Quakers.

The Last Days of New Amsterdam

Things seemed to be going well
in New Amsterdam in 1664.
The streets were in better condition.
Stuyvesant was improving the schools.
He had appointed "overseers of bread"
to keep the food supply pure.

Most of the rich people built
their houses on Broad Street.
Some of our modern buildings
look like the early Dutch houses.
One of them is this Brooklyn
bank building.

Suddenly the Dutch rule ended! A British fleet
sailed into the harbor and demanded that the colony
be given up to the English. Stuyvesant wanted to fight,
but the Dutch West India Company had not sent him
enough guns or soldiers. The people of New Amsterdam
would not fight. Many of them thought they would be
just as well off under British rule. So poor, bossy,
brave Peter Stuyvesant had to surrender. The city
of New Amsterdam became the city of New York.

"Old Silvernails" went back to the Netherlands.
Later, he returned and lived on his farm, called
"bowery" in Dutch. A street was named The Bowery,
after the lane that led to his farm.

New York as an English Colony

"You have a good understanding of the Indians and the Dutch in our city," said Mr. Park. "You are ready to find out what things happened after the Dutch days. How will you plan your unit?"

The children decided to get as many pictures as possible. "You can't find photographs of New York in the early days," Mr. Park told the children. "People didn't learn how to take photographs until about a hundred years ago. But you can get copies of old drawings and paintings."

"We can write stories of things that happened, also," said Betty. "Or we can find good stories to read from books. Will you tell us stories of happenings we can't find in our books?"

"Of course," said Mr. Park. "To start off, I will give you a story of New York City under the English. The English ruled here for more than a hundred years.

"The Dutch were not unhappy under the English. Things changed very little. But one thing bothered the older Dutch people. As time went on, the young people began to speak English. This led them to go to English churches instead of Dutch ones.

"Only one thing could be done. The Dutch churches would have to use the English language instead of the Dutch. That is just what they did. At this time the city had been English about a hundred years.

"The city grew rapidly under English rule. In 1730, about the time of this picture, it had between eight and nine thousand people. Notice the British flag on the ship and the other one on the fort. The British had given the Dutch fort a new name, Fort George, after their king.

"In 1790 the city had almost four times as many people as in 1730. Yet it was small compared to the cities of today.

"People had less liberty in those days than we have today. For one thing, they could read only good things about the government. Newspapers did not dare print a word against any British governor. But at last some New Yorkers started a newspaper to tell the truth about a bad governor. This paper was called the *New York Weekly Journal*.

"The printer of this paper was John Peter Zenger. He was a brave man, who had agreed to take the blame for the articles against the governor. For a year he was allowed to print the paper. During that time, the readers of the *Journal* were learning how important a free newspaper was. Then Zenger was thrown into jail, where he was held for almost a year. His wife kept on printing the paper.

"When Zenger's case came to trial, the governor would not allow New York lawyers to defend him. An old lawyer from Philadelphia came to New York to defend the printer. The lawyer, Andrew Hamilton, made a fine, strong speech about freedom to publish the truth. Then the case went to the jury. No doubt many of the men on the jury had read the *Journal*. They understood the importance of freedom. So they brought in a decision of *not guilty*.

"The people of New York shouted with joy at the jury's decision. They lifted the old lawyer on their shoulders and carried him down the steps of City Hall. The case was a victory for Peter Zenger and for the people of New York, past and present. The freedom of American newspapers to print the truth dates back to this time."

Pictures told some other facts about New York under
English rule. The boys and girls of the committee
had written captions for each picture. Here are
the pictures and their captions:

Near the Perine House
on Staten Island stands
this old tree. The house
was built about fifteen years
after the English took
New Netherland. This tree
was probably brought from
England and set out
when the house was built.

This picture shows
the kitchen and dining room
of the Perine House. What
old-fashioned objects
can you find in this room?

This is the Perine House as it looks today.
New parts have been added, but the old part
still stands. Can you guess which is the old part?
The big tree is behind the house. You can visit
the Perine House, but you must get permission
a week ahead of time.

Bushwick Church was in Bushwick village. What does
the signpost at the right say? Look at the map of Brooklyn
to find Bushwick, and Newtown Creek.

Early churches had eight sides so that the settlers
could defend themselves from all directions. In case
of Indian wars, the settlers might gather in the church
for better protection.

This stone church in Flushing, Queens, was finished in 1699. The English used it for twenty-six years. As you know, many English people had settled in Queens even during the Dutch days.

In 1704 a road through Brooklyn called the King's Highway was begun. Passengers and mail crossed the East River from Manhattan on the Fulton Ferry. A stagecoach was waiting near the ferry to carry them down the King's Highway through Flatbush to New Utrecht. They crossed to Staten Island by another ferry. From Staten Island, they were ferried to Perth Amboy on the mainland.

Did you ever stop to pay toll when driving on a highway? The plan is not new. There were toll roads in colonial days. Notice that in this picture the tollhouse is built right across the road. This tollhouse was in Jamaica, Queens.

The Voorlezer's House was a Dutch schoolhouse on Staten Island. This wooden building has been standing here since before 1696. It may be the oldest school building for young children still standing in the United States. Meanwhile, the fine Dutch houses of brick on Manhattan have all burned or been torn down. Can you guess why the Voorlezer's house is still standing?

The people of the Dutch Church wanted their children to go to school so that they could read the Bible. They did not have much money, so they often built one house to be a church, a school, and a home for the schoolmaster. In the Voorlezer's House, you can see the rooms for each of these uses.

The Voorlezer was a church worker as well as a schoolmaster. Voorlezer is a Dutch word meaning *reader* or *before reader*. He read the Bible to people on Sunday *before* the minister arrived. (Oldtime ministers often had two or more churches in different villages. They might have to be rowed across New York Bay to get from one church to another.)

The Voorlezer had other duties. He rang the church bell, led the singing in church, and kept people quiet while the preaching went on.

You can visit the Voorlezer's House by making plans ahead of time.

Can you guess what
the boys and girls
are carrying? What story
does this picture tell?

The boys and girls sat
apart and recited lessons
at different times. In
what ways is this
schoolroom different from
yours? How do you think
the room was lighted
on dark days? How was
it heated?

The girls are having
their singing lesson.
They are probably singing
church songs.

This picture shows how fire fighting was done about 200 years ago. The fire chief, who is in front of the fire engine, shouts orders through his trumpet. What do you think the people with bags and baskets are carrying?

The largest building in this picture was the first Methodist church building in America. It stood on the south side of John Street in lower Manhattan. The picture shows the street in 1768. How had people's clothes changed since Dutch days?

The Blue Bell Inn was
built on Manhattan Island
before the Revolution.
How has the lady traveled?
The gentleman? Do you know
what the trough beside
the porch was used for?

A moving picture theater,
the Coliseum, stands
in the Blue Bell Inn's place
today, on 181st Street.

This is Lefferts Manor,
a Brooklyn farmhouse, built
about 1777. The house is
larger and better built than
Van Twiller's farmhouse,
built about 140 years
earlier. This house may be
seen today in Prospect Park.

In Indian and colonial times, whales were
often seen in New York Bay and the Hudson River.
In fact, the Dutch tried to start a business
in whales, but did not succeed. The English
went after whales that were washed ashore.
Whale oil was used in making candles.
The Indians were given the tail and the fins —
the parts of the whale they wanted most.

Ann's committee read its report. Some parts were from books, and other parts had been written by the children. The topic was

The Revolutionary War in New York

Our city has taken part in everything important that has happened in our country. In colonial days each colony worked more or less by itself. But when trouble started with England, the motherland, the colonies began working together. England made laws to control the ocean trade of the colonies. The laws were good for England but bad for the colonies, especially those with big harbors. The colonies wanted these laws changed. Many Englishmen agreed. Friendly Englishmen got the bad laws changed, but then new ones were passed. King George and his friends would not listen to our complaints. English soldiers were sent to see that the King's laws were obeyed.

Many people in New York wanted the laws changed, but they did not agree about what to do if King George refused. Some people thought that the colonies should stick with the motherland no matter what happened. Others thought that the colonies must become independent.

Little fights started in some cities. New York City was the place where the first blood of the Revolution was shed. It happened during the Battle of Golden Hill in 1770. Within a few years, England and her colonies were at war.

In 1776 many American leaders got together and signed
the Declaration of Independence. People were wild
with joy when they heard the news. Church bells rang.
Men and women cheered, and you can be sure that
the children cheered louder than anybody else!
Liberty poles went up in many a village square.
As our country had no flag yet, the liberty poles
were decorated with small banners. These banners
had patriotic words and sayings on them.

A liberty pole standing today in New Utrecht,
Brooklyn, is especially interesting. It is
the sixth one that has stood in the same place.
As the older ones blew down, new ones have been
put up by the New Utrecht Liberty Pole Association.

When New York City heard of the Declaration
of Independence, men and boys hurried to
Bowling Green, in Manhattan. There stood
a huge statue of King George. This picture shows
what happened to it.

Every town and village in what is now New York City
had something to do with the Revolution. First of all,
the British sent many troops to Staten Island. Here you
see the British ships sailing in through the Narrows,
as they were seen from Staten Island.

Before long the British crossed the Narrows to Long Island, near Fort Hamilton. Washington and his men were in camp on Brooklyn Heights.

The English followed several roads in marching toward the American camp. There was fighting near the Red Lion Inn and at other points along the roads to Brooklyn Heights.

The Americans were no match for the well-trained British troops, who had many years of experience. Our soldiers were mainly farmers and city workers who had been in the army only a few months. But they were very brave.

A small group under General Stirling took a stand in an old stone house. They kept the British busy while the rest of the Americans escaped to Washington's camp. But only ten of Stirling's group got back to the American camp. The rest of his men were killed or taken prisoner.

If the British had attacked the American camp right then, they probably could have taken it. The war would have been lost, because about half of the whole American army was there with Washington.

But luck was with us. The British waited. Meanwhile, Washington planned a way of escape for his men. Down the cliffs of Brooklyn Heights they crept by night. Below them, in the East River, waited every patriot who had a boat in New York harbor. There were big and small boats, rowboats, fishing boats, ferries.

Silently, the patriots rowed the escaping Americans to Manhattan. Some officers kept the campfires burning to the last, to fool the British. Then they went away, leaving all Long Island in British hands.

As soon as any land fell into British hands, there was a search for men who had signed the Declaration of Independence. A man from Whitestone, named Francis Lewis, was one of the signers. When the Flushing men could not hold back the British soldiers, the British sent some horsemen to Whitestone to capture Lewis. He was not at home, but his wife was captured and his house was burned.

Mrs. Lewis died soon after her release from prison. After the war, Francis Lewis was so sad about what had happened that he did not go back to Whitestone to live.

The American troops, having escaped from Brooklyn, were defeated in Manhattan. Most of them reached Harlem Heights, safe but sad. Next morning they drove back some British troops and began to feel better.

But it was impossible for the Americans to hold out against the large British forces. Washington sent the greater part of his troops to the mainland north of Manhattan. The force he left at Fort Washington was defeated. This picture gives an idea of the battle, as if you were seeing it from University Heights in the Bronx. Large rowboats are carrying British soldiers across the Harlem River to Manhattan. Fort Washington is on the high ridge in the center. There is a small park in this place today.

The loss of Fort Washington left Manhattan to the British. The Bronx could no longer be held. Washington and his men withdrew to New Jersey. There were American posts north of New York, but all the city was in British hands. And so things were until the end of the war.

Pablo's committee reported on this topic:

The Revolutionary War Is Over!

New Yorkers were glad when the war was over. But there were new problems to meet. Now that our country was independent, it had to learn to govern itself.

Wise men got together and wrote the Constitution. In 1788 it became the law of the United States.

All Americans were happy to have the problem of government settled. Every city had a celebration. New York had one of the best, with a big parade. A make-believe ship paraded as a symbol of the Constitution. It was the Ship of State, which would carry the country safely into the future. From its deck, men made speeches. A New York hero was Alexander Hamilton, who had worked hard to get the Constitution accepted.

George Washington and New York City

Did you know that New York was the first capital of the United States? When George Washington became our first president, he lived and worked in New York.

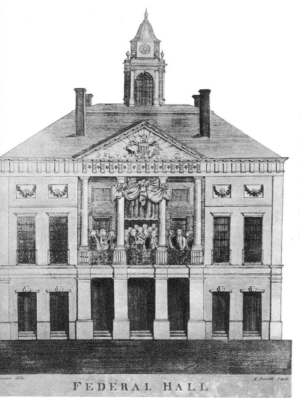

FEDERAL HALL

Here is a picture of Washington taking the oath of office as president. The building had been the latest City Hall, but the city gave it to the new United States government. Its name was changed to Federal Hall, and our first United States Congress met there.

Federal Hall no longer stands. In its place is a building now used as a museum. Washington's statue stands where he took the oath of office. This building is right in the heart of Wall Street, a center of banking and business.

President Washington usually went to church at St. Paul's Chapel. This picture shows it about forty years after Washington's time, when there was more traffic on Broadway.

St. Paul's is the oldest church still standing in Manhattan, and one of the oldest buildings of any kind in our country. It was built before the Revolution, in 1764. That was just a hundred years after the British took New York. If you visit this church, you will find a surprise: its steeple is at the back. Inside, the church looks very much as it did in Washington's day.

While Washington lived in New York, he had to have an operation. In those days, doctors did not know about the drugs that can put a person into a deep sleep. Washington, like other people, just had to take the pain of his operation. He was very brave.

People loved him so much that they wanted him to have quiet while he was getting well. Therefore, they stretched chains across the streets so that traffic could not pass his house. They spread straw on the other near-by streets so that Washington would not hear the *clop-clop* of the horses' hoofs. Would straw help much nowadays?

At this time Washington lived in Franklin Square, but New Yorkers were getting a fine home ready for him. They hoped that the government of our country would stay in New York. So they called this home Government House.

At the same time some people thought that Morrisania (now part of the Bronx) would be a fine place for the nation's capital. Still others thought Brooklyn Heights would be a beautiful location.

Washington never lived in Government House. In about a year the government moved to Philadelphia. It stayed there while the brand-new city of Washington was being built for our nation's capital.

The people of New York City were sad when Washington left. They were sorry that the city was no longer the capital of the United States.
But at least New York was the capital of New York State for a while. The governor lived in Government House. This picture was taken from a water color painted several years after Washington left New York.
Notice the cows lying peacefully in the driveway.

The United States Customs House stands in the place of Government House today. No cows here now! From the Customs House steps, you can look up Broadway at this view.

The statue you see is in Bowling Green. Early in the Revolution, Washington stayed about where number 1 Broadway is today, at the left of Bowling Green.

Joan's committee read a story about

New York After the Revolution

New York City was a sad sight right after
the Revolution. Twice during the war great fires
had raged here. Nobody knew what had caused them.
The British blamed the Americans, and the Americans
blamed the British. No matter who caused the fires,
the black and ugly ruins cluttered the city.
Everyone was glad that St. Paul's still stood.
The citizens had fought hard to save it.

The largest buildings still standing were dirty
and in need of repairs. Many had been used as prisons
for Americans soldiers captured in the war. Others
had been used as barracks for British soldiers kept
here to hold the city.

American prisoners
of war were also kept
on British ships
in the East River.

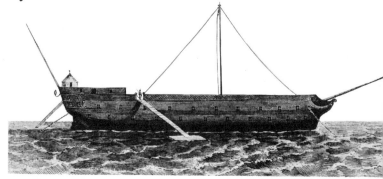

Once the war was over,
New Yorkers began cleaning
up their city. Streets
were cleared of blackened
rubbish and brick. Many
new buildings went up.

At this time New York had only 33,000 people, but it was growing. New Yorkers were worried because the streets were crooked. Some streets had two names. Besides, the houses had no numbers.

People did the best they could in numbering houses on the old streets. Then they made a plan for new streets all the way up to Spuyten Duyvil. The streets were to be straight. They were to have numbers instead of names. The short crosstown streets were to make square corners where they met the long up-and-downtown avenues. That is why it is easy to find our way around Manhattan today. However, we can run into trouble where Broadway crosses these well-planned streets.

Broadway goes uptown at an angle. Wherever it crosses an avenue, it makes a triangle. Union Square, Times Square, Lincoln Square, and many others are really triangles caused by Broadway's wandering.

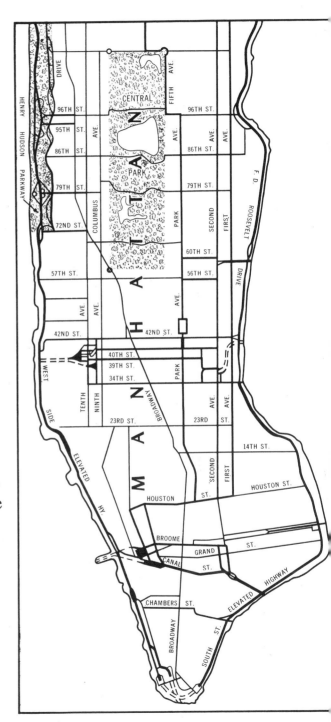

New York wanted to be pretty as well as easy to travel in. "Way uptown" — from 47th to 51st streets — the New York Botanic Garden was laid out. Rockefeller Center stands in this place today. If you have ever been skating at Rockefeller Center, you have been right where these old flower gardens were.

Rockefeller Center has some beautiful gardens of its own. Every Christmas the gardens have splendid Christmas displays.

You might like this dramatic view of Rockefeller Center as it would look if you saw it straight up.

This view is from Chambers Street in 1808. The big building in the center is the city prison. At the left is the City Hall, not yet finished. The building in front of the prison is a school for poor children. (There were no public schools in those days.) Notice the small white building at the right. It is the Office of the Board of Health. This was the beginning of our great Department of Health, which now is in this modern building.

The snow scene is a picture of Greenwich and Warren streets in the early 1800's. Would it be safe for you to go sled riding in the streets near your home?

A few years later a water color
was painted of Broadway showing
the new City Hall. Here is a copy
of it. At the left you can see
one pillar of St. Paul's Church.
Broadway is quite different today,
but City Hall looks the same.

Farther uptown and in all the other
boroughs, there were only farms
and villages. There were country houses
and mills, like this one in the Bronx.
The zoo of Bronx Park is on this land
today.

This snow scene in Brooklyn, painted in 1817, shows a good-sized village. Rows of houses line the streets, and there are many people around. Yet in some ways this is like a country scene. How? Can you find the boy pumping water for his horse?

Near the streets was a ferry landing. The ferry carried people, animals, and goods between Brooklyn and Manhattan. Many years later, Brooklyn Bridge was built to take the place of the ferry. Some of these streets were destroyed or changed to make way for the bridge.

Here is a modern scene of the land under the Brooklyn tower of the great bridge.

Transportation Helped the City Grow

New York is located on the greatest harbor
in the world, and ocean trade has helped our city
to grow ever since the Revolution. By 1817
packet ships were sailing between here and Europe
at regular dates. Today we send all sorts of things
abroad — wood from our forests, foods grown on our farms,
goods made in our factories.

New York has always been a great city for travel,
too. Americans going to Europe pass through the city.
Most people coming from Europe land here first.
Even in the Dutch days, eighteen languages could be
heard on New York streets. People of every religion
came to New York because they had more freedom here
than in most places. They came also for a chance
to earn more money and to make better homes
for their children.

Everything that has made transportation quicker
or safer has helped New York to grow. In 1807
Robert Fulton invented the steamboat. He was living
in New York at the time, and he first tried out
his steamboat on a trip up the Hudson to Albany
and back. His little boat, the *Clermont,* took
five days for the round trip. But sailboats took
twice as long, so Fulton's invention was a success.

Soon many ships began using steam. Steam engines
could move ships without the help of wind and tide.
But for a long time ocean ships kept their sails
in addition to the new steam engines. Steamship travel
between here and Europe began in the middle 1800's.
Here is the *Britannia,* an early English steamship.
It took her two weeks to cross the Atlantic. How long
does it take a liner today?

Better ships would be coming. But another
transportation problem was troubling New York City.
This problem troubled all parts of our country
that had goods to ship from our harbor. This was
the problem of getting the goods to New York.
There were no trains and no trucks to move
heavy goods, such as lumber and meat. Goods
from the West could be carried on the Great Lakes
as far as Buffalo. From there they had to be loaded
into wagons that horses would pull across the state
of New York to Albany. The roads of dirt,
or sometimes of planks laid crosswise, were not good.
Carrying goods by land was the hardest part
of the trip. At Albany the goods could be loaded
onto boats again for the trip downriver to New York City.

Some wise men had a plan for a canal that would
carry goods across New York State. Our governor,
DeWitt Clinton, thought the plan was good. Some other
people did not, because digging the canal would cost
a good deal of money. But Clinton won out.

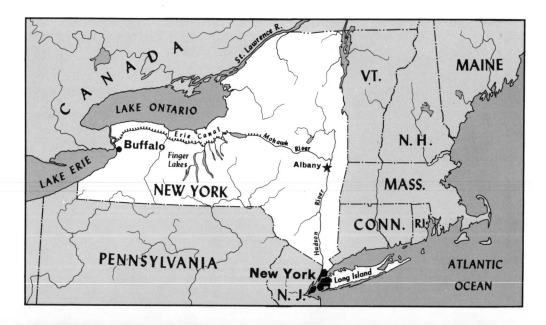

It took eight years to dig the canal. Two thousand
men worked at it, among them a large number of Irish
who had just come to America. The canal is still in use
today, although trains and trucks have taken away
much of its trade. There are good songs and stories
about the early canal days. Try to find some of them.

New York City had a great celebration in 1825
when the canal was finished. The news came by cannon.
A cannon was shot at Buffalo when the canal was opened.
Farther east, a gunner with another cannon heard
the first shot and then fired *his* cannon. So it went
all the way across New York State and down the Hudson.
New York City got the news in eighty-one minutes.
How would such news be brought to us nowadays?

Brightly painted boats started from the Lake Erie end
of the canal for the first trip. These boats had
no sails nor engines. Horses or mules walking along
the banks pulled the canal boats by ropes. Clinton
and other people who had planned for the canal rode
on these boats all the way to New York City. It took
them three and a half days to get here. How fast
can the trip be made today?

When Clinton's boat arrived, he lifted a keg
of water he had brought from Lake Erie. This water
he poured into New York Bay for a "wedding"
of the two great bodies of water.

The city went wild with excitement. Cannons
were fired. People shouted and waved flags.
A parade five miles long went to meet the governor.
All the important groups had a part in the parade.
The fire companies had some very exciting displays.

The canal helped New York City just as people
had hoped. Now it cost six dollars to bring a ton
of goods from Buffalo to New York. Before the canal,
it had cost a hundred. More goods meant more trade.
More trade meant more jobs. By the time the canal
was a year old, five hundred new businesses had been
started in the city.

New York was no longer a baby among cities. By 1820 it was larger than Philadelphia. It kept growing as more and more people came from Europe to live in the United States. In 1825, twelve thousand came. In 1836, there were seventy-five thousand new arrivals. Many of them stayed in New York.

In the 1830's New York's finest homes looked like the ones in this picture of lower Broadway. Notice the bus that carried people around town in those days. The bicycle had no pedals. You pushed it along with your toes.

The man driving the cart with the barrel on it brought good drinking water to anybody who would buy it by the gallon. New York City's water came from springs and wells. Some of the water was not safe to drink. There was hardly enough water for the city's drinking and washing.

Things look happy and peaceful in this picture, don't they?

However, life here was not always peaceful. The city had many problems. In a way, it was growing too fast.

Men were in such a hurry to put up new buildings that they sometimes built carelessly. This picture shows a store that fell down before it was even finished. Our buildings, with their steel framework, could not go to pieces as this one did. But even they must be well built.

The problem of caring for the very poor was great, but not much was done to help them. Their clothes were hardly better than rags. They hadn't enough food to keep them healthy. Their homes were often wooden shacks crowded together in dirty streets. Fires and dangerous sicknesses often swept through poor neighborhoods.

Families who had just come from Europe usually had to live in the worst neighborhoods. Some never made enough money to move away. Others got jobs, worked hard, and moved to better homes.

In those days, children were allowed to have jobs. This newsboy of the 1840's probably had no schooling, but we may be sure that he had learned how to make change.

The Problem of Water

New York's impure water caused diseases. The lack of water also brought great danger in case of fire. After the Great Fire of 1835, the city decided to bring water from the Croton Lakes.

It was 1842 before the great Croton water system was finished. When the clean water came pouring into the city reservoir, everybody was excited and happy. There were fireworks and speeches.

In City Hall Park a fine fountain was waiting for Croton water. When it came gushing out, a great shout went up. A parade marched past the lovely sight. How are the onlookers dressed? Had styles changed much since the Revolution?

The reservoirs that received Croton water first were in what is now Central Park. One of them is still there. The water was sent to another reservoir, from which it was piped to all Manhattan.

The reservoir for sending water out to the city was at Forty-second Street and Fifth Avenue. As you see, it had a walk at the top of its wall. Here New Yorkers could stroll to enjoy the view and the cool feeling that the water gave them.

Our great public library today stands where the old reservoir stood.

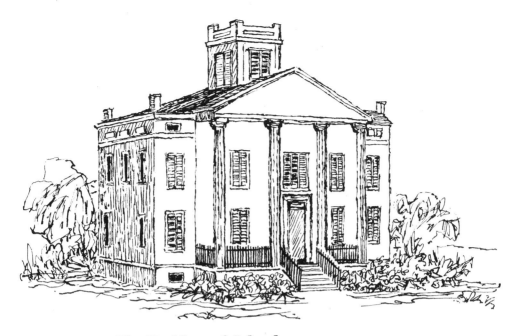

The Problem of Schools

After the Revolution there were two kinds
of schools in the city. Children went
to private schools if their parents were rich.
Other children went to schools that the churches
set up for their own pupils. This is a picture
of a private high school for girls from rich families.

A child whose parents were not rich and did not
belong to any church had no chance to go to school.
People worried about these children. What kind
of life could they hope for without education?
Would they be able to earn a living? Would
they even know the difference between right and wrong?

A group of men decided to set up a free school
for the education of poor children who did not
belong to any church. The youngest children usually
went to school in the basement, boys and girls
together. The older boys and girls were not taught
in the same rooms; there was a floor for boys
and a floor for girls.

This is a picture of a school for little children. All children were in one huge room, so that one teacher could take care of them. The youngest sat in rows of steps, one above another, at one end of the room. The children marching are saying their 2's table in a singsong, "Twice one's two, twice two's four."

The racks in the center were used to show the arithmetic, reading, or spelling lessons to be studied.

The free schools had many pupils. However, a good many children were still getting no education. Why? They and their parents were proud. They felt that they would be like beggars if they attended schools that they did not pay for.

The public school plan ended this problem. Schools were to be for every child, rich or poor. The money to pay for school buildings and teachers was to come from taxes. The State of New York joined with the governments of cities and towns to take charge of the schools. Many children still went to private or parochial schools, but every child had a right to go to public schools.

A Hundred Years Ago

Mr. Park's children wanted to know what our city was like a hundred years ago. "A good place to find out," Nora said, "is the Museum of the City of New York." So the class went to visit this museum.

Best of all, the children liked the collection of toys and dolls that children of long ago played with. There was a doll's house built to look like a brownstone house of a hundred years ago.

page 61

"A hundred years ago there were no apartment houses," Mr. Park said. "Many New Yorkers lived in houses of this sort, which were built side by side in a solid row. Row houses are still often used as homes in Manhattan and Brooklyn.

"In spite of the row houses, Manhattan and Brooklyn had many countrylike things about them. For instance, wagons such as this brought fresh milk to city people every day. This delivery man let his little girls ride with him sometimes."

The children liked the picture of the Crystal Palace,
a great building of glass and iron. It was built
in 1852 as a home for a world's fair. It stood just
back of the reservoir between Forty-first and
Forty-second streets. Mike was interested
in the transportation people were using — a bus,
a horse car, and a private carriage.

New York has had other
world's fairs since that
of the Crystal Palace days.
Today we have a fine
new building for fairs.
Do you know where it is?

After their trip to the museum, the children wrote
a story about life in New York a hundred years ago.
They illustrated it with pictures from museums.
Here are some of the things they told:

New York was a great port
in the 1850's, as it still is.
This picture of the Narrows
shows you how many ships
were entering and leaving
the harbor then. Packet ships
came regularly from Europe
bringing many immigrants.
Clipper ships sailed to China,
as well as to California.
How do people usually go
to California today?

Did the factories of the 1850's look like
today's? Coal was used for power, so New York's
smoke problem was beginning!

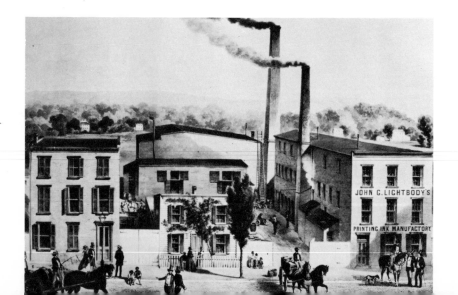

Schools like this were in use in parts of the city where people lived close together. This is a school in Williamsburgh, a part of Brooklyn. The picture was drawn by a boy of thirteen.

This picture shows a child's room of a hundred years ago. What do you like about the room?
How is it different from yours?

The children's book had a chapter on
Central Park
A hundred years ago our city planned a great park. It was to cover the land from 59th to 110th streets and from 5th to 8th avenues. Since it was almost in the middle of Manhattan, it was to be called Central Park.

Central Park might not have been finished so soon if there had not been bad times in 1857. There was a depression like the one in the 1930's, with many men out of work. In 1857 the city government put jobless men to work making Central Park.

Horsecars such as this were soon running uptown to the park. How many people do you think the car might have carried?

The first picture shows Central Park in the old days. The second picture shows the park nowadays.

Mr. Park helped the class with the next chapter. He explained about

New York and the Civil War

New York City has always been interested in things that happen in the United States. Just before the Civil War, New Yorkers were especially excited. All over the country Americans were worried about slavery. Those in Northern states thought that slavery was wrong. Those in Southern states thought that they could not get along without slaves.

In Brooklyn there was a preacher who hated slavery. His name was Henry Ward Beecher. After his sermon one Sunday, Mr. Beecher said, "Sarah, will you please come here?" From somewhere in the church came a beautiful young colored woman.

Mr. Beecher said, "Sarah is a slave. Do you think we can collect enough money to buy her from her owner?" He told the story of Sarah's struggle for freedom. Soon the people in the church were sobbing. They threw money and jewelry into the collection baskets. Enough money was collected to buy freedom for Sarah and several other slaves.

The slavery question brought our country to Civil War when Abraham Lincoln was president. The North and the South fought each other. Many brave men from all over the country enlisted as soldiers.

As soon as the war started, the women of our city got busy to help the soldiers. In those days there was no Red Cross, so the women collected money to send nurses for the soldiers. They sent bandages and other comforts for the wounded. They held great fairs in Manhattan and Brooklyn to raise money. With the money, they helped the wives and children of men wounded or killed in the war.

New York City cared for people who had fled from the South, both whites and Negroes. The city sent doctors and teachers to the South to help the slaves who had been freed. Thanksgiving dinners were sent to soldiers in the field. Food was sent even to Southern people, when New Yorkers heard that they were starving.

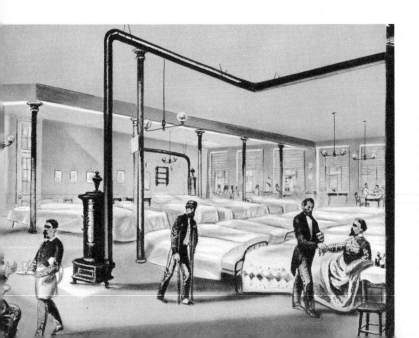

New York City had hospitals for the wounded. This picture shows you one of the hospitals. How is it like the hospitals of today? How is it different?

New York made many of the things needed in the war.
The Brooklyn Navy Yard made and repaired ships.

NAVY YARD, BROOKLYN, N. Y.
VIEW TAKEN FROM THE EAST SIDE OF WALLABOUT BAY, WILLIAMSBURG.

The Navy Yard had got its start in 1801.
Up to the time of the Civil War, it had
made ships of wood. But now it made
an ironclad battleship, the *Monitor,*
which took an important part in the war.
The Brooklyn Navy Yard is now the largest
in our country. Among the great ships
it has made is the aircraft carrier,
the *Missouri.*

New York had many war troubles. Spies came
into the city. After Lincoln was elected president
for a second term, the spies plotted to start riots
in the largest Northern cities. They did not get
far with their plot, but they did set fires
in several New York City hotels.

In 1865 the Civil War was over. The North had won. Slavery was done for. Then, one day, terrible news came to the city. President Lincoln had been shot! Amid all our happiness about victory, the man who had planned that victory lay dead. All businesses closed, except stores that sold mourning clothes. Black flags hung from business buildings and homes, rich or poor. Church bells were rung in slow, sad notes.

The body of the president was brought to New York. For twenty-four hours it lay in City Hall. Thousands of New Yorkers came to pay their respects to Lincoln. Then the body was taken to the railroad station. The funeral procession starting up Broadway is shown in this picture. What does the picture tell you about people's love for Lincoln?

A few days later Rosita read a story about

New York After the Civil War

In the years after the Civil War, many business streets of the city had trees to shade the sidewalks and awnings to keep the buildings cool in summer. The highest buildings had only three or four stories.

Buildings like these were soon going to look low, for an eleven-story building went up in 1889, at 50 Broadway. It had a steel frame, but even so people were afraid such a tall building wasn't safe! The man who had planned it took an office on the top floor to show that he was not afraid. From that time on, buildings were built higher and higher.

High buildings would not be any good without some way to get to the top. The steam-powered elevators right after the Civil War carried people up only five or six stories. That was as high as was necessary then.

When buildings became taller, elevators had to change, too. New inventions made it safe for elevators to rise higher.

Street Transportation

New York City was growing fast. Buses and horsecars were drawn by horses and were rather slow. The Broadway buses rumbled along in an almost solid line, not more than thirteen seconds apart. But still they could not take care of the crowds. The people who couldn't find seats hung on by straps.

In winter big sleighs took the place of buses on some streets.

Horsecars ran on rails, and gave a smoother ride. They looked like small trolley cars inside and outside.

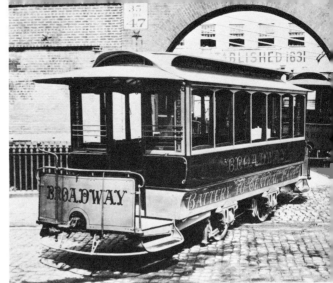

A few horsecars were furnished like sitting rooms. People paid extra fare to ride on these special horsecars. In what ways do you think this car was better than regular ones?

Railroad trains, from faraway and near-by towns, ran through Manhattan streets to three stations downtown. Although they were forced to move slowly, they were always causing accidents. So, by 1875, the New York Central was running underground from 42nd to 100th streets, just as it does today.

In Brooklyn, which was not so crowded, trains still ran at street level. They were used to take people from one part of the town to another. Horsecars and steam trains shared the same tracks.

Finally somebody got the bright idea of putting railroad trains on elevated tracks. Soon after the Civil War, the first elevated railroad was built on Greenwich Street in lower Manhattan. As you can well guess, people were scared of riding on thin, shaky stilts. At first the elevated was not a success.

The builders of the elevated thought that New Yorkers were scared to see anything so heavy as a steam locomotive overhead. So they enclosed the early locomotives in pretty cars, like the fancy one shown here. But before long, people got used to the elevated, just as you someday may get used to rocket ships. They could get to work and back home again much faster.

When the people got used to the elevated, the fancy outside was taken off. The locomotives then looked like this one.

First, the Ninth Avenue elevated line was built,
then the Third, Sixth, and Second Avenue lines.
Brooklyn also soon built elevated lines, and lines
went to the Bronx. The steam locomotives burned coal,
and had a bad habit of blowing out smoke and cinders
every so often. The hot cinders and dirt and dust
would drop on people walking in the streets.
No wonder that New Yorkers were still not happy
about their transportation.

At this time there were
no automobiles or trucks.
City departments still had
to depend on horsepower.
Steam fire engines had been
invented, however, and they
pumped water through hoses
faster than the strongest
and bravest men could do it.
In 1865 the city had its
first paid fire department.

How do you like this way of cleaning streets?
The sanitation man still had to work the slow way.

The Brooklyn Bridge

At the end of the Civil War, New York City
(then only Manhattan) had about three quarters
of a million people. For many years it had been
the largest city in the United States. Brooklyn
was the third largest. It had joined with some
smaller near-by towns to become a city in 1834.
The two big cities helped each other in many ways.
New York people got food from farmers in Brooklyn.
Many Brooklyn people worked in New York.
Fifteen ferry lines carried people and goods
across the East River from one city to another.
But safer, quicker transportation was needed.

So the two cities decided to build a bridge across
the East River. John Roebling, an engineer who had
built other great bridges, was given the job of
building the new bridge. Just as the work was
to begin in 1869, Mr. Roebling died from an accident.

His son, Washington Roebling, carried on
the work according to his father's plans.
One of his helpers made a trial trip across
the river on the first loop of cable strung
between the two towers. Amid cannon shots,
whistles' shrieks, and people's shouts,
he made the round trip in 22 minutes.

It took about fourteen years to finish
the Brooklyn Bridge. Two other bridges
have been built since then to connect
Manhattan and Brooklyn. However,
Roebling's bridge is still the most famous.
Now it is always called the Brooklyn Bridge.

Communication Improves

Communication was changing as fast as transportation. The telegraph had been invented by Samuel F. B. Morse some time before. The first message was sent in 1844. The telegraph was a great success.

This picture was made in 1880. By that time, telephone wires had joined telegraph wires to darken lower Manhattan streets.

Alexander Graham Bell invented the telephone about ten years after the Civil War. At first, most of the telephones used were in business places. There were only 252 names listed in the Manhattan telephone book of 1878. Numbers were not given. You asked the operator for the name of the person you wanted. (All the operators were men, by the way.) Can you guess how many names there are in the Manhattan book today?

In March, 1888, a terrible blizzard, with heavy snow and strong winds, struck New York and all the country round about. Many people were stranded because transportation was held up. Streets were blocked all over the city. People ran out of food, milk, even coal to keep them warm.

This picture shows you what the Great Blizzard did to telephone and telegraph poles. Overhead wires had long been a danger in crowded areas. Fire or wind could bring down the poles, and then the electricity in the wires was a danger to people and animals. The blizzard made people realize that overhead wires were too dangerous to allow. As a result, wires were run through pipes and placed underground. By 1893 wires in the more built-up parts of the city were all underground.

Education and Enjoyment

New York City was becoming more and more a center of education and enjoyment. There had been libraries since colonial days. King's College, founded before the Revolution, later became Columbia. Soon there were other colleges.

In 1874 the first building of the American Museum of Natural History was begun. The Metropolitan Museum of Art was founded in 1880. Three years later the Metropolitan Opera Company was founded. Brooklyn had its Academy of Music, and both cities had a number of theaters.

Not everyone in New York, however, was getting his share of education and enjoyment. One hundred thousand New York children were working in factories all day long. The Children's Aid Society held night schools, where these children might get some education.

Of course, many people were making a good deal of money. Broadway crowds looked like this.

Mike's grandfather, Mr. Murphy, came to tell the class what New York City was like when he was young. At first, he explained

The Turn of the Century

The turn of the century is the time near the end of one century and the beginning of the next. I remember when the 1800's turned into the 1900's. I suppose I was dressed like the boy in this picture.

You will see the turn of the next century. It will be an especially exciting one. After 1999 ends, the year will be 2000, and the date will start with a 2 for the next thousand years.

New Things on Wheels

My friends and I thought the beginning of the 1900's was exciting. For one thing, transportation was changing so fast. We were excited because electric trolleys were replacing horsecars. The first ones were no bigger than horsecars.

Larger ones were soon built. The closed trolleys, like 289 in this picture, were better the year round. The open ones were cool. People liked to ride in open trolleys in the summertime.

I used to take the trolley to ball games.
My favorite team was the New York Highlanders.
They later became the Yankees, and I'm sure
you boys know their home park.

Electric trolleys made traffic
more dangerous, because they
scared the horses. I remember
Union Square in the old days.
It was so dangerous that it was
called "Dead Man's Curve."
There were no traffic lights.
The police had a terrible time
directing traffic. People kept
rushing in front of trolleys,
horsecars, buses, and carriages.
At certain times of day,
of course, the traffic was not
so bad.

I can remember back when
the first subway was started.
It was the IRT. In 1900
the first tunnel was built
in front of City Hall.
From City Hall station,
the line ran north
to Forty-second Street.
There it turned west
to Times Square, then
north again and up Broadway
to 145th Street. This line
opened in 1904. In about
a year there was a line
to the Bronx.

The subway soon burrowed under the river to Brooklyn.
But there was some trouble in ventilating the tunnel.
The subway company decided to build a ventilating shaft
near the Brooklyn end of the tunnel. The shaft would
come out of the ground on a pleasant street
of Brooklyn Heights. The neighbors said, "We won't
have an ugly ventilating shaft on our nice street."
After a long argument, the subway company bought
one of the homes on this street. They tore out
the inside of the house. Then they installed
ventilating machinery and steel stairways
to the tracks. It looks just like a house, but if
you knocked at the door, nobody would answer.
Only subway workers go into this house.*

* If you turn to the picture on page 62, you will see the house
that hides a ventilating shaft. Can you tell which one it is?

I shall never forget the first automobile I ever saw. It looked strange, but my friends and I thought it was wonderful. Early cars were not comfortable, fast, or even safe. Some were driven by steam, some by electricity, and some by gasoline engines. At first only the rich could afford them. In time they were improved and became cheaper, too. Soon quite a few were seen on New York's streets.

There were trucks and motor-driven buses, too.

Here is Fifth Avenue in 1908. How is it like a winter snow scene on Fifth Avenue today? How is it different?

But I must get back to the turn
of the century. We all still
enjoyed quiet, dreamy pleasures.
On summer evenings, we sometimes
went riding on the swan boats
that glided over the lakes
of the big parks.

When I was a boy, my friends and I liked to ride
our bicycles to City Island. It was a peaceful place,
where fishermen, oystermen, and pilots lived. There were
shipyards on City Island, where pleasure boats were built
and repaired.

In 1910 I found a new way to go to City Island.
I took a small electric trolly car at the Bartow
railroad station. Instead of having two tracks
and a single trolley wire, this car had a single track
below and two above. Four little "ears" held her
to the overhead rails and kept her steady on curves.
We called her the Flying Lady because she almost
had to fly to keep her balance. Nothing on wheels
could keep up with her in those days.

Why isn't she still racing to and from City Island?
One day her motorman slowed her down on a curve.
And that was the end of the Flying Lady.

Builders think the idea of this little trolley car
was all right. But her track and her overhead supports
had been put up in a hurry and with cheap materials.
And besides, she couldn't go slow!

You might be interested to know that single rail trains are used today in Germany. Other types are being planned here. The one in this picture is being planned for San Francisco. Do you suppose New York will ever have single rail "els"?

"That story shows how the present comes from everything that has ever happened," Mr. Murphy said. "The future will come from the present and the past, too." With that he went on to talk about

More Light!

The coming of electric lights was another important change. When I was young, the streets were lighted with gas lamps. In some parts of town a lamplighter would go around each night lighting the gas street lights.

Here is a picture of the first
station New York had for generating
electric current. You might compare
it with the newest one, which is
in Astoria.

At first the wires to carry electricity for lights
were strung overhead on poles. But before my time
Edison had found a way to send electricity safely
underground. By 1917 some streets looked like this
when the pavement was taken up. What is inside
the pipes? One of the diggers said he should use
a spoon instead of a shovel. Can you think why?

Buildings and the People That Use Them

The first skyscrapers were exciting. One was called the Flatiron Building. It was built in 1905 and was the highest building of its time. But not for long! The Woolworth Building soon made it look hardly middle-sized. How does each of these buildings compare with today's skyscrapers?

Many people were already living in apartment houses at the turn of the century. On the edges of all the boroughs people lived in countrylike houses. I lived in this big wooden house.

My family and friends had a pleasant life. However, we knew people who didn't. These people often lived in crowded, dirty, unsafe neighborhoods. They had so little money that they could not pay for homes in good neighborhoods. Some of the people had just come to our country from Europe. The fathers and mothers had the worst jobs with the smallest pay. They had so little money that it was hard for them to keep themselves or their children healthy.

Here we see a visiting nurse for the Department of Health. She visited poor people who had sickness in the family. She also visited mothers and showed them how to keep their babies well-fed.

In the early 1900's the schools tried to help with health problems. The Little Mother's League trained big girls to take care of younger children. The Department of Health sent nurses to inspect children in schools. This is true today, but the nurse's job is not so hard as it once was. Then there were many more children with troubles such as mumps or eye diseases.

The children who were ill and those who had serious hurts were sent to the school doctor.

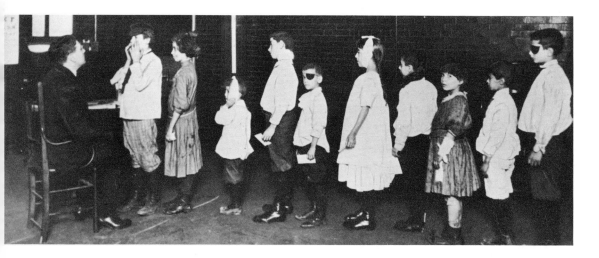

Since those days our city government has done much to help people help themselves. National and state governments have done their share in making a better life for more people. Labor unions have helped, too. Housing projects have been built to replace many of the tumbledown houses.

Mike's grandfather was about to close his talk. Then Mr. Park asked, "Aren't you going to tell us anything about the beginning of Greater New York in 1898? We would like to hear the story from someone who was around at that time."

"All right, then," said Mr. Murphy and he told how

Many Different Communities Became One City

Nothing was changed for me. My part of the Bronx had voted to join Manhattan 'way back in 1874. Then in 1895 the rest of the Bronx was added to New York. Here is what Franklin Avenue and 166th Street looked like in 1898.

It was hard for Brooklyn people to decide to make their city part of a larger one. Brooklyn had a million people and was one of the largest cities in the United States.

Brooklyn people were proud of their history. All the other villages that had made up King's County in 1683 were now part of Brooklyn. The county had been named after Charles the Second, who was King of England when it was formed.

Many old Dutch place names still are used in Brooklyn. If an old settler should return to Brooklyn today, he would know some of the names on the subway signs.

Well, all the old villages were now to be part of New York. To this day some Brooklyn people think the whole idea was a great mistake. But Brooklyn is doing well. It now has nearly three times as many people as when it joined Greater New York — more than Manhattan or any other borough. It has more than 7,000 factories. It carries on more than half the shipping trade of the entire port of New York.

Queens County was named after King Charles' wife, Queen Catherine. The County of Queens became the Borough of Queens when it joined New York City.

Queens had only one city, Long Island City, when it became part of Greater New York. It had eight villages. It began growing faster when the Queensborough Bridge, connecting it with Manhattan, was opened in 1909. It grew even faster after the subway and elevated lines reached it. People who worked in Manhattan were glad to find that they could now live in Queens, part of which was real country.

Today the Whitestone Bridge connects Queens to the Bronx, and the Triborough Bridge connects Queens to the Bronx and Manhattan. Cars and trucks can pass through the Midtown Tunnel to and from Queens and Manhattan.

There are twenty-one bridges that link Manhattan to other parts of the city. Here are the Williamsburgh and Manhattan bridges. What boroughs do they connect?

Since 1898 New York has been a city of five boroughs — Manhattan, Queens, the Bronx, Brooklyn, and Richmond. Except for London, it is the largest city the world has ever known.

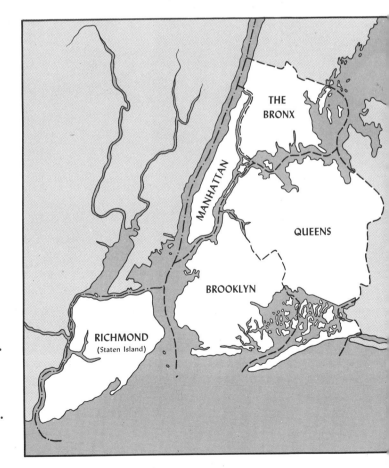

THE
BRONX

MANHATTAN

QUEENS

BROOKLYN

RICHMOND
(Staten Island)

The parts of the city were quite different in 1898. Some boroughs had crowded streets. Every borough had farms and villages. This picture shows a well near a country home in upper Manhattan.

This first picture shows you a Brooklyn school at the turn of the century. The second shows a school in the Bronx, built a few years after Greater New York began. How is the Bronx school like your school? How is it different?

Mr. Murphy had spent almost the whole day talking with the children, answering questions and showing them his pictures. They thanked him with words, smiles, and hand clapping. Some of them had another idea, but it was still a secret.

A few days later Mr. Park gave a little talk on

The Meaning of History

Everything we see has its history. Some trees
and springs we find in the wildest parts of our parks
were here in Indian days. Most of the springs
and streams have been covered by pavement. Drains
and pipes had to be put in to carry the water away.
Otherwise, the water would have flooded basements
and made pavements sink.

The ocean, the bay, and the rivers are almost
the same. The shores may have different shapes,
because of made land. Lower Manhattan, south of
Pearl Street, is made land. Flushing Meadow Park
and the park along Riverside Drive are on made land.
The Department of Sanitation makes land by dumping
old rubbish, called landfill, on marshy land
or in shallow water near shore. When the landfill
is built high enough it is covered with earth
and planted.

The harbor itself is
much the same. We owe
to it our great growth.
But without people to use
the harbor in new ways,
it could not have become
so important. The city
and many companies
have built huge piers
to handle goods.

page 95

The land around the harbor looks different from the way it used to look. Name some of the man-made things you can see in this picture of the harbor.

The people of New York City all have their part in our city's history. Maybe their families came here with the first Dutch or the early English. Maybe they came as immigrants from Ireland or Italy, Germany or Russia in the middle or late 19th century. Maybe their parents or they themselves have come lately from other parts of our own country. Were you or your parents the first ones of your family to become New Yorkers? Or did your grandparents or your "great-greats" choose New York as their home?

People are still coming here from the Old World, but not nearly so many as used to. People come from the New World, too — from the West Indies, South America, Mexico. Many come from Puerto Rico, which is now part of the United States.

The people who came here were of many religions, and New York has all kinds of churches. It has churches for people of many languages.

In the early Dutch days
Jews came here. At first
they were allowed to worship
only in their homes. But
this rule was changed,
and today there are
temples in every borough.
This temple is in the Bronx.

The Dutch, who founded the city,
were Protestants, and the colony
in the early days was chiefly
Protestant. Today many different
groups of Protestants have churches,
large or small, in our city.

Great numbers of Catholics came
in the 19th century. For a while
Brooklyn had no Catholic Church.
Good Catholics of Brooklyn used to go
across the East River to attend Mass.
In fact, many religious groups
in newer communities used to go
to other boroughs to attend church.

Every man-made thing in our city has its history. Many of the public buildings have a long history. A church may stand on land where earlier churches of the same religion burned down. Some old church buildings are used by a different group from the one they were built for. The people of the older group moved away and sold their building to newcomers. One old church has become a storage warehouse. It looks very strange to see arches and church windows in a warehouse!

Today we think our Grand Central Station is beautiful. In 1871 New Yorkers were just as proud of their new station that stood in the same place.

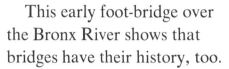

This early foot-bridge over the Bronx River shows that bridges have their history, too.

There was usually an earlier bridge, or a ferry line, in the same place as today's modern bridge. For instance, the Bayonne Bridge between Staten Island and New Jersey replaced a ferry line.

The government of our city has its history, too. The office of mayor started when the British took the colony. But even in the Dutch days, we can see the beginnings of city departments. The Rattle Watch did one of the jobs our Police Department does.

Early fire fighters worked hard, but they were not professionals using good equipment. There was no professional fire department until 1865.

On those days and for a long time afterward, firemen were using the kind of equipment shown in this picture.

What protection we have today!
Searchlights show where
the great streams of water
should go. Ladders can rise
safely into the air without
leaning on anything.

The Fire Department also has
rescue companies. And, as
the greatest harbor in the world,
it has fireboats.

Transportation in the city changes
with the times. Buses have taken
the place of trolleys. On Manhattan,
subways have taken the place of
elevateds. The old elevated lines
darkened the streets, but made
interesting designs of light
and shade.

In parts of Brooklyn,
Queens, and the Bronx,
the subway runs on overhead
tracks.

New types of subway cars
are often put into service.

Nowadays our city government needs many things from other parts of the United States and even from all over the world. The Department of Purchase had this float in a parade not long ago. The map of the United States shows where automobiles, oil, and other things come from. The figure standing on the float is Father Knickerbocker. He is the symbol of New York City.

Today Sanitation trucks keep our city's streets clean. Of course, the trucks can't do the job by themselves.

At the turn of the century The Department of Sanitation was worrying about rubbish on the street. This picture shows you why. Before and since then, the department has been trying to get people interested in keeping the streets clean. Clean City Leagues for Children are sponsored by the department.

Sanitation has always been important in our city. It has much to do with health. Garbage collection has been a problem since early days. Remember how Peter Stuyvesant hated having pigs let loose in the streets to eat food scraps?

In 1805 a garbage collector went around lower Manhattan with his cart, ringing a bell to get customers.

More than a hundred years later, men were still emptying garbage into horse-drawn carts.

Today workers still have to handle garbage, but they are helped by machines that pull the garbage into the big Sanitation Department trucks.

Our city government did
not get motorized trucks
very early. Here we see
how the Sanitation men
used to remove snow.
Notice how the first
snow plow was fastened to
the front of an automobile.

The Department of Health has many new duties.
It now gives children polio shots. It sends men
to inspect many kinds of food brought into our city,
and to make sure the food is fresh and good for us.

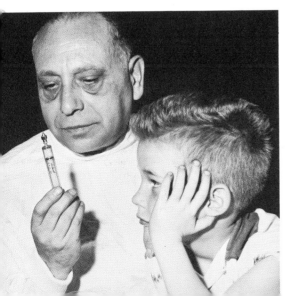

The Health Department
has well baby clinics
today just as it did
around 1900. Babies are
better cared for now,
but department workers
are still busy wherever
they are needed.

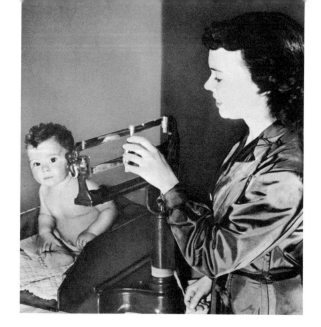

The Department of Police
is always doing something new.
Today mothers are trained
by the Police Department
to be school crossing guards.
They do very good work.

The Transit Authority has
something new all the time.
One new thing is "the subway
that goes to sea," the line
that goes to Rockaway Beach.
This picture shows you
the trial trip.

This picture gives you an idea
of the closeness of Brooklyn
and Manhattan. It shows
the Brooklyn entrance to one
of the tunnels that burrow
under New York Bay to Manhattan.
Cars and trucks use this tunnel.

The ventilating tower for the tunnel is near
Governor's Island. Have you heard that the water
between Governor's Island and Brooklyn is called
Buttermilk Channel? The Dutch settlers gave it
this name, probably because the water, foaming up
so white, reminded them of buttermilk.

Look again at the picture. Straight across the bay
is New Jersey. Did you know that the Dutch West India
Company claimed New Jersey as part of New Netherland?
When the British took over, they made New Jersey
a separate colony. So today we have two states,
New York and New Jersey, that share the port of New York.

New York City's Board of Education has a long history.
You have seen pictures of schools of long ago. Here is
a picture of one of the newest ones, in Queens.

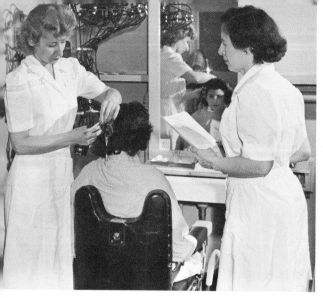
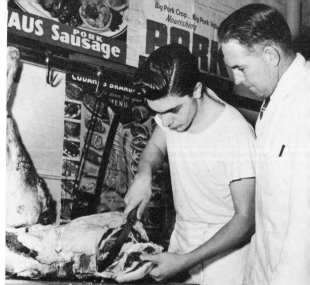

New York's schools give education in many kinds
of work that were not taught in schools a hundred,
or even fifty, years ago. High school pupils learn
how to wave hair, cut meat, bake bread, decorate
fancy cakes, and do many other jobs.

Some city departments that were not
thought of in the early days have been
started. One department has the job
of keeping the air of the city clean
from factory smoke, bad odors
from automobiles, and other impurities.
Men from this department have a way
of deciding how bad the smoke is,
as you can see here.

The Department of Markets tries
to see that people get a fair deal
when buying. This collection
of unfair scales will be destroyed.

"Mike's grandpa told us such interesting things that happened when he was young," said Don. "Our parents have told us things, too. Mr. Park, will you please tell us what happened when *you* were growing up?"

"I will," Mr. Park said, and he began telling

What Happened Day Before Yesterday

My father was too young to fight in World War I, but I had an uncle who told me about going off to Europe in 1917. From the port of New York soldiers from this city and from all over the country sailed to Europe. A great many of them returned here after the war.

My mother and father were married in the 1920's, after the war. They had everything they wanted, even one of the first radios. Money was easy to earn, and easy to spend. Like everybody else, my parents thought that good times would last forever.

But suddenly everything changed. Wall Street banks and businesses were no longer doing well. Businesses began to fail everywhere. Many people who had been rich became poor.

Some men who had had good jobs now sold apples on the streets. Others stood in lines to get food that was given out by churches, labor unions, or other groups. It was a sad time — this time of the Great Depression.

I was very young during the worst of the Depression,
but I was old enough to be a soldier in World War II.
Our country entered the war late in 1941. It was the first war
in which American women had been in the armed forces.
In fact, I met my wife in the war. We were stationed
at the same army post in the Pacific.

How happy we were when we returned to New York!
But we had trouble finding an apartment. The building
of homes all over the United States had almost stopped.
Most factories and many men had been used to protect
our country. After a while, building began to catch up
with the needs of families. We got an apartment
in a housing project.

A very important happening near the end of the war
was the start of the United Nations. This was a group
of nations that hoped to keep war from coming again.
New York City was chosen to be the place where people
from all over the world would meet to talk about
United Nations business. The United Nations buildings
now stand in the mid-Forties, near the East River.
A meeting of the General Assembly is pictured here.

We were in New York — and so were you, of course —
when the last elevated line in Manhattan was
torn down in 1955. Here is a picture of the station
at Third Avenue and Forty-second Street, which was
one of the last to go.

Many new things are always happening in New York.
Soon our city may have atomic plants for peaceful uses.
Probably we shall see many earth satellites in the
near future. You can be sure that New York will not
miss much that is exciting.

Some of the changes may seem strange as strange
can be, but you will find that they too have
a history. Always remember that

Today Came from Yesterday

"I like this history unit," Abe said. "Wherever I go,
I try to think what the place was like long ago,
a hundred years ago, and just yesterday."

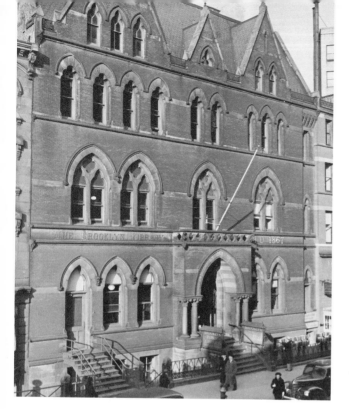

"I went to the library last week," said Jane. "My dad told me that it was the first central library in Brooklyn. It was built soon after the Civil War.

"Our new central library is very modern. But probably it is no more so than the old one was in its time."

"There are new things to see all the time," Jim said. "Last Sunday we went driving through the Holland Tunnel. The traffic policeman rode in a little car on a catwalk above the road. Dad said that these policemen had to walk until a short time ago."

"I went to Staten Island to see my grandpa last week,"
said Rosa. "I went all through the new ferry house.
Here is a picture of it. It shows a ferry starting out.
You can see Governor's Island beyond the ferry."

John said, "Last Saturday I enjoyed our ride
over the George Washington Bridge. Dad said that
many people like to live in the country and still
work in New York City. The city would have
fewer workers without bridges, tunnels, and ferries.

"This picture shows the George Washington Bridge
from the west."

Morris said, "My brother Joe is learning to be a member of the Merchant Marine. He spends some of his time in high school working on the schoolship *John W. Brown*. The boys who work on the *John W. Brown* do not take trips, but they learn all they can while in harbor."

Mr. Park said, "My wife and I live in Queens. Queens is the aviation center of the world. It has two huge airports, LaGuardia and International.

"The world's best tennis players come to play in tournaments at Forest Hills in Queens. The race tracks at Jamaica and Aqueduct are famous.

"Queens has many factories, too. The borough is a center of the electronics industry. Various foods are made in our big plants. In the days before radio and TV, a great many homes had pianos. A large number of these pianos were built in Queens. Steinway Street was named for one of our famous piano factories.

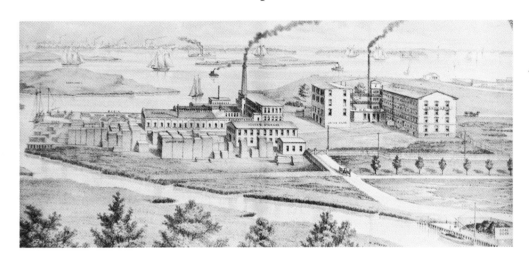

"Many industries are located along Newtown Creek. This waterway, which forms the boundary between Queens and Brooklyn, is one of the busiest waterways in the United States. Can you find the oil refinery at the top left? Here is how this refinery looked seventy-five years ago.

"There are many things to tell about every borough. Who would like to tell us about the Bronx?"

"I would," said Phil. "My cousins live there, and they know every inch of Bronx Park. They have shown me all sorts of interesting things, such as the Rocking Stone. This stone can be moved even by a child, but it doesn't tip over.

"Of course, the zoo is my favorite place in Bronx Park. You can see the animals living in the open there."

"I love simple little homes such as this one," said Mary. "A great American poet lived in this cottage when he was young and very poor. His name was Edgar Allan Poe. He wrote mystery stories as well as poems. My sister likes Poe's mystery stories."

"My father teaches at Fordham, a college in the Bronx," said Tim. "The Bronx has many colleges, both public and private.

"The Hall of Fame is on the New York University campus. Great Americans of the past and present are honored there."

"I love Manhattan," said Betty. "We take out-of-town visitors there to see the sights. We took my cousins to see Manhattan at Eastertime. They enjoyed watching the helicopters land on the roof of a building.

"Their most thrilling sight was the Empire State Building at night. The lights of Manhattan look like magic at night.

"We stood in front of a glass bank building on Fifth Avenue and looked and looked. We could see everything that went on inside. It seems strange to have a modern building that isn't a skyscraper, doesn't it?"

Nick said, "I used to live in Manhattan. My friends and I liked to go to Central Park. We could play games, sail our boats, or visit the zoo.

"On Sundays we sometimes walked
along Park Avenue with Mother
and Dad. The New York Central
railroad runs right under it.
Dad said that in the old days
this part of the city was covered
with railroad yards."

"Manhattan has one especially interesting school,"
said Mr. Park. "It is for children who are actors,
singers, or dancers on the New York stage. They have
odd hours of work and have to spend much time
rehearsing or taking lessons. This school has
shorter hours than your school, but to make up
it has small classes and much special help.
The children can go to this school until they are
ready for college. If the young performers have
to travel, they get their lessons by mail.

"New York has always been noted for its theaters with 'live' shows. Of course, soon after moving pictures were invented, there were movie theaters all over the city.

"Here is an old movie house in Queens. Compare it with the ones you are used to. Some of the first moving picture studios were in Brooklyn."

"Well, I'm glad I live in Brooklyn," Harry said. "I like Prospect Park, especially the zoo. And best of all, I like Coney Island.

"Coney Island has a new aquarium, and people from all over New York visit it. They visit our beaches, too."

New York Tomorrow

"I wonder what New York will be like when we are grown up," Charlie said.

"It will surely be different," said Betty. "But I think it will still be wonderful to live in."

"I agree," said Mr. Park. "New York changes all the time, but much of it stays the same. We have past and present always with us here.

"For instance, Columbus Circle has both the Columbus monument and the Coliseum. The first is a statue of the man who, in 1492, gave America to the world. The second is America's new building for world trade fairs. This picture of both is really two pictures, one placed on top of the other to show the old and the new together."

"I saw a doorless door that gave me some idea of the future," said Joan. "The door is only a beam of air flowing downward, which keeps the cold outside in winter and the heat outside in summer. There is a real door that closes when the business day is over."

"I saw a cartoon about a new way of cleaning the subway," said Morris. "It showed giant vacuum cleaners on a flatcar. My grandmother says the subway hasn't been cleaned since it was built more than fifty years ago. She hopes this vacuum will do the job!"

"Maybe it will. If it doesn't, no doubt someone will think of a better idea," said Mr. Park. "Right now, we have to think of the *near* future. What ideas do you have on closing your unit on HOW OUR CITY GREW?"

"Some of us have been talking about that," said Pablo. "We hope the rest of the class will agree with our plan. We would like to make pictures and models of New York City, old and new. We want to invite Mike's grandfather, Mr. Murphy, to be our guest of honor. He taught us *so* much."

Mr. Park liked the children's idea very much.
A few days later Mr. Murphy was the guest of honor
at the art display called

Yesterday and Today in New York City

One committee had done a history
of the lot where the school stood.
Indians, of course, had first used
the lot. The children could find
nothing about the lot after that
until it was used as a coal yard,
about a hundred years ago.

Then a countrylike school was
built on the lot.

Their own school was built
about fifty years later.
Since then, it has been
cleaned and made more modern.

Another committee gave a report on famous buildings of New York City. A third committee reported on how city departments have grown.

The fourth group made models of homes in New York from the earliest days. Here is their model of a modern apartment building.

Mr. Murphy liked the children's display. He said, "You say I taught *you*. But you have taught me a good deal about
THE BIG CITY
AND HOW IT GREW."

To the Teacher

The Big City and How It Grew is one of a series of books for children to read in connection with social studies units. Others in the series touch on one or another aspect of city history, past or present, and may be consulted for further information.

The content of *The Big City and How It Grew* is appropriate for various age levels. The vocabulary and sentence structure have been kept as simple as possible in view of the nature of the facts and ideas to be presented. Illustrations in profusion will help children to gain accurate concepts of life in different times. Though designed primarily for the independent young reader and the retarded older reader, the book offers much to children whose immaturity or reading disabilities limit them to studying the pictures and listening as the text is read aloud. This book can be useful to seventh graders who are unable to read the textbooks on New York City's history designed for their age level. Many of the activities and experiences suggested in the following pages may be adapted to various age groups and enjoyed by both readers and non-readers.

THE PURPOSE OF THIS BOOK

This book will help children to develop a friendliness toward history. It tries to impart a sense of the flow of the past into the present and of the present into the future.

The city's history is arranged here on a straight chronological thread. Those events that promise to be most interesting and comprehensible to children are highlighted. The great national and international events in which our city played its part were included for the sake of the children's sense of history. Children must realize that New York City rallied to the impact of the Revolutionary War, the Civil War, and the two world wars. The city was involved in the Industrial Revolution, the Great Depression, the founding of the United Nations, and the beginning of the electronic-atomic age. Some of these developments are touched on only lightly and in less formidable language; but all are present, either explicitly or by implication.

The authors felt that the chronological approach is more easily understood by most children. The teacher who, however, prefers to start with the known and work back to the unknown may trigger this approach in any way she thinks best and then help her children get their backward look from the facts presented here.

Since an understanding of history is always interwoven with an understanding of geography, this book plays up knowledge of New York's geographical advantages. There are simple maps to illustrate the verbal explanations.

Dates are used throughout the book as pegs on which to hang events and developments. It is expected that children will memorize dates only when dates are essential. It is generally recognized that the time concepts of fourth-grade children are fairly primitive, and learning to repeat dates in a parrotlike way will not result in understanding.

CONCEPTS TO BE DEVELOPED

Some concepts are stated directly in the text. Others will be developed through discussion. Concepts arrived at through experience and discussion are more likely to remain with children in a functioning way rather than those merely memorized.

Concepts that should develop through activities centering around this text include:

Places have stories. The true story of a place is called its history.

The history of a place usually tells us about the people who have lived in or near the place. The history of a place changes as new people come or earlier people go away.

New York City has an interesting history. It is now the biggest city in the United States. Its history tells why it grew so big. All the people who have lived here have changed the city in some ways. People came here from all over the world to help make the city. They became Americans and New Yorkers.

People have come here because of where

New York is. It is on a great ocean harbor and also on a great river.

New Yorkers of long ago were much like New Yorkers today. They lived on the same land, got fish from the same waters. All needed homes, food, and clothing. All had some kind of education and some kind of religion. All had ideas of liberty and justice.

However, the New Yorkers of long ago were different from us in some ways. In what ways did their foods differ? Their clothes? Their homes?

The people who lived in our city before us did and made many things that have helped us. They built bridges, churches, public buildings, and homes. They founded businesses in which people still work. They insisted on being free and passed on to us their ideas of freedom. They improved schools; created parks and museums for our pleasure; planned ways to help more people live in health and happiness; and planned better care for people unable to take care of themselves.

New York has been one city since 1898. Although each borough has a different history, the city of today belongs to everybody, no matter where he lives. Every New Yorker may be proud of the fine things about all the boroughs.

CONCEPTS REQUIRING SPECIAL ATTENTION

The fact that New York in Revolutionary days had quite a large proportion of Tories may come as a shock to some children. Some of the people who were against the war recognized that the colonies had been badly treated by King George; they were in favor of trying to get justice, but they did not think that it was right to break away from the mother country. When the colonies won the war, some people, still loyal to England and to the King, moved away to England or to Canada. Others stayed here, and became loyal Americans.

The concept of freedom of religion may not be easy for children to grasp. Teachers may help children develop it by pointing out the variety of churches and synagogues in the neighborhood.

The concept of freedom of the press may also require some explanation.

The idea of New York City as a gateway, a crossroad, and a stopping point may be developed through facts about family background that children report and through explanation and extension brought in by the teacher.

SUGGESTED APPROACHES

The approach to the study of the city's history should be through experiences in the children's daily living. Some such approaches may be:

historical anniversaries celebrated in the local community or in the city;

a visit to a landmark of interest;

a census;

a special historical exhibit at a museum;

a radio or television presentation of an historical incident.

HISTORY AS STORIES

History is appealing to children when it is presented as stories of places and of people. Following are some stories that supplement the text:

The Battle of Golden Hill (January, 1770) was a fight between British soldiers quartered in New York and patriotic citizens. It is regarded as part of the Revolution for the same reason that the Boston Massacre is—it was an event leading to the War. Since it occurred several weeks earlier than the Boston incident, it is claimed as the first instance of bloodshed in the Revolution.

The cause of the conflict was the destruction of the fourth liberty pole set up by the Sons of Liberty in the common (now City Hall Park). Three had been destroyed by British soldiers (or "persons unknown"). The fourth pole was secured with iron. The soldiers tried to destroy it on four different nights. At last they succeeded, and sawed it up into pieces that they piled up near the meeting place of the Sons of Liberty. Not content with this insult, they put up posters abusing the patriots. From this provocation, trouble arose; and at the corner of John Street, then called Golden Hill, soldiers fired on the crowd, who defended themselves with clubs and canes.

The Battle of Pell's Point was an incident of the Revolution in which a group of American soldiers in the Bronx held off a much larger number of British, who had walked into a trap. This victory saved Washington's army from destruction as it retreated through the Bronx to White Plains. The site of the battle is now marked by a big boulder called Glover's Rock (for the colonel whose 700 men defeated 4,000 British), in Pelham Bay Park. A mural representing the incident may be seen in the Bronx County Building.

Giving the houses street numbers was a necessary job. Without numbers, you could explain where you lived only by saying something such as "near the shoemaker's on Wall Street." But making a plan for street numbers was hard. Some streets went wriggling around corners. These streets had once been paths made by people who, naturally, turned aside for hills, swamps, streams, etc.

GOOD SOURCES OF INFORMATION

The teacher may find the following sources of information useful:

The Columbia Historical Portrait of New York, by John A. Kouwenhoven. Garden City, New York: Doubleday & Company, 1953.

The Memorial History of the City of New York, edited by James Grant Wilson. (History to 1892; 4 volumes; can be found in libraries.)

History of the City of New York, by Mrs. Martha J. Lamb and Mrs. Burton Harrison. (2 volumes; available in libraries.)

ACTIVITIES TO HELP CHILDREN DEVELOP A SENSE OF HISTORY

NOTE: Many appropriate places to visit are listed in *A Guide to Some Educational Resources in the City of New York,* Board of Education, 1954.

Visit Stuyvesant's grave, in the churchyard of St. Marks on the Bowery.

Visit the Voorlezer's house. Compare its surroundings with those of the early Dutch houses shown in pictures of lower Manhattan.

Visit (at the same time as above) St. Andrew's Church, near the Voorlezer's house.

Visit the Perine House; notice rooms and furnishings of different periods.

Visit City Hall Park and its environs, including St. Paul's Chapel, Trinity Church, and the Federal Hall Memorial Museum.

Study the history of various types of transportation. Individuals, or groups, particularly boys, may be interested in collecting pictures of old steam locomotives, automobiles, steamships, etc.

Ask parents and/or grandparents about earlier transportation in New York.

Discuss customs of necessities that have persisted over a period of time: as strap-hanging on horsecars, trolley cars, buses, subway trains; government's protection of the food supply (from Stuyvesant's "overseers of the bread" to our Department of Health).

Learn and sing some songs of early Erie Canal days. Read or tell stories of canal builders or travelers.

Children competent and interested in research may like to find out the difference between packet and clipper ships; methods of safeguarding pedestrians; traffic cops, traffic lights, "Walk" and "Don't Walk" signs; early plans for a subway; etc.

Local interests should be developed; for example, Brooklyn children will be interested to learn what villages became part of Brooklyn, which were Dutch and which English. The history of the community should be studied. The history of a local building, bridge, library, square, or celebration may be investigated.

Write imaginary diaries of boys or girls living at different periods of the city's history.

Let each child study his own family's relationship to New York: when the first ancestor (or present generation) came, why (if the reason is one easily and willingly told), where the family has lived, what the members have done (business, political offices, etc.). Take a poll of the class, or possibly of the school, to find where the parents of the children came from. (Born in New York City? Continental United States outside of New York City? Puerto Rico or other possessions? Foreign lands?)

Study the history of your school and its site. The cornerstone of the building may help, as well as a tablet to be found in most schools, telling the date of the building. Earlier use of the site may be found by consulting old inhabitants, records in near-by libraries, or real estate records.

Discuss: Will the history of today be easier for children of the future to study than the history before 1850 is for us to study? (The thought to be drawn out is the change that photography—still movies, television—has made in the clarity with which we can see events. Earlier events and customs, including some pictured in this book, are represented only by imaginative paintings or drawings which, although based on the best available information, are not as reliable as photographs.)

Plan and produce puppet shows or dramatizations to illustrate events or ways of living during New York's history.

Let committees choose a city service of interest, and make slides or pictures to show the progress of this department or agency, from colonial days to the present.

Let every member of the class contribute to a master list of books, recordings, songs, stories, and poems having to do with New York City.

Children may study the seal or flag of New York City, of their borough, or of any other appropriate unit. The Queens flag is used here as an example of the meaning that seals or flags have if properly understood: The blue and white stripes were copied from the shield of Kieft, who bought the land that is now Queens from the Indians. The circle stands for a string of wampum, because the Indian name of Long Island, Sewanhaka, was taken from the Indian word for wampum (sewan). Why? The red and white rose on the flag stands for England, and the tulip, for the Netherlands. The crown stands for Queen Catherine, for whom the county was named Queens. The flag of Queens shows respect for people and groups who have helped make its history.

Let gifted children decide what New York City was like at the turn of the century, in 1600, 1700, 1800; and compare with what it was like in 1900 and what it may be like in 2000.

Study buildings in the neighborhood that may be typical of various periods studied.

ACTIVITIES TO HELP CHILDREN DEVELOP CONCEPTS OF THE GEOGRAPHY OF THEIR CITY

Talk about the kinds of maps with which the children are familiar. What are the points played up in each kind (road and subway maps, political, physical, topographical) and what are the uses of each?

Make maps of the schoolroom, the school, and the school block.

Learn geographical terms applicable to New York City and its environs: river, ocean, harbor, coast, valley, lake, bay, island, hill, Palisades, the Narrows, etc.

Study maps of New York City and its neighboring states and bodies of water. Learn about the boroughs, the bridges important to the immediate community and any other distant ones which children may visit, tunnels, parks, and other features.

Study the globe and world maps to discover the relative size of New York harbor, its position in relation to other continents, continents from which it is most likely to receive people or goods.

Make maps (three dimensional if practicable and useful for the purpose to be served) showing items of interest to the children, such as transportation lines, parks, museums, etc.

Make a class bulletin board display, or a class picture folder, to show interesting features of New York City.

Plan a big pictorial map showing places of interest in New York City. The places may be represented by original artwork or by photographs, magazine or newspaper clippings, etc.

Prepare a picture file on New York City today.

Take boat trips to the Statue of Liberty and to Staten Island, to clarify ideas of the harbor.

Take bus trips to see various sections of the city: business districts, as Wall Street; neighborhoods to which groups, as Chinese, Italians, Germans, have given their imprint; port areas, as Battery Park with its view of the Statue of Liberty and the West Side Elevated Highway with its view of the big piers and the ships at berth.

Encourage children to take trips with parents: boat trip around Manhattan, and visits to famous landmarks of New York City, airports, museums, Grand Central Terminal (guided tour available), Erasmus Hall High School, Bowne House, etc.

ACTIVITIES TO HELP CHILDREN UNDERSTAND THE CITY TODAY

Each child may make a painting or crayon drawing showing what most appeals to him about the city today.

Children may give talks or write explanations on: What makes New York a great city.

Make posters with slogans to urge people to keep the city clean.

Make posters to attract visitors to New York City.

Let the class make a master list of the most important buildings, monuments, parks, amusements, industries, and points of interest in the city.

Make a list of the city's leading important citizens.

When maps, pamphlets, and the like are needed, class members may write to the Port of New York Authority, the New York City Chamber of Commerce, the New York Convention and Visitors Bureau, or other agencies.

Children may watch for appropriate programs on WNYE, WNYC, and other radio or television stations—for historical, geographical, or other information on the city; listen to programs telling how boys and girls can make best use of the city's recreational and educational facilities; give oral reports on various sections of the city in which they have lived or where they have visited and tell how these places differ from their home community.

The teacher may select and show to the class interesting audio-visual materials relating to New York City today.

Word List

WORDS WHICH MAY NEED TO BE TAUGHT, WITH NUMBER OF PAGE ON WHICH EACH FIRST OCCURS.

The publishers express their appreciation to the following for permission to reproduce the photographs on the pages indicated.